Siimon Reynolds *young success sto..... .. ..,* *Siimon had co-founded, built and successfully sold three advertising agencies, including one in New York. He is a winner of the International Advertising Association Scholarship, and was awarded New South Wales Young Achiever Of The Year in the career section.*

Now thirty-three, Siimon is currently co-owner of VCD, voted 1997 Advertising Agency Of The Year. In his spare time Siimon studies human potential, and has given speeches to over 50,000 people on this subject.

Other books by Siimon Reynolds in Pan:

Become Happy in Eight Minutes

when they zig, you zag

Siimon Reynolds

PAN
Pan Macmillan Australia

First published 1998 in Pan by Pan Macmillan Australia Pty Limited
St Martins Tower, 31 Market Street, Sydney

Reprinted 1998, 1999, 2000

National Library of Australia
cataloguing-in-publication data:

Reynolds, Siimon.
When they zig, you zag: how to achieve health and
happiness by doing the opposite to everyone else.

ISBN 0 330 36080 9.

1. Happiness. 2. Self-actualization (Psychology). I. Title.

158.1

Typeset in 14/18 pt Bodoni by Post Pre-press Group, Brisbane, Queensland
Printed in Australia by McPherson's Printing Group

To George, King of Zag.

INTRODUCTION

I have studied successful people now for over 15 years.

While they may differ in age, race, occupation and motivation, I have realised that great achievers all have one thing in common.

They travel their own road.

They think differently than the average person. Feel differently, act differently and so their achievements are fundamentally different, and greater.

If you accept that the average person rarely achieves excellence, then if you seek greatness it makes absolutely no sense to do what the average person does.

The gold medal in life always goes to the contrarian. The man or woman with the guts to dance to their own tune, to step out, to risk, to ignore the jeers from the crowd on the sidelines and walk (as Scott M. Peck so eloquently put it) the road less travelled.

This book is for those who understand that if one lives a life like the masses, one will never rise above the masses.

It's full of simple yet powerful ways you can act and think differently to everyone else, and thus change your life for the better.

It's a book for champions, and champions waiting to be.

Be clear about what you value in life.

Do you value health over success? Family over career? Business over friendship? Spirituality over social life?

What are your values?

Most people don't have a clue.

As a result they live wishy-washy lives, devoid of clear direction and power.

As Confucius once said, 'He who aims at nothing . . . is sure to hit it!'

Take half an hour to think about these areas of your life, and then list them in order of importance: Business, family life, social life, health, spirituality.

Which is number one in importance? Which is number five? Once you've worked out what you value most, ask yourself whether you are currently living your life in accordance with that values ladder.

If not, change your life.

Living a life according to your values is truly one of the great secrets to happiness.

To stay young drink more water.

Dehydration is believed by experts to be one of the major causes of ageing. Not only will you look old if you don't drink much water (your skin becomes wrinkled), your kidneys will be less able to eliminate impurities efficiently.

Even brain cells are affected by dehydration. According to longevity expert, Professor Stanislaw Talalas, the average person loses about three litres of water a day. So drink at least two litres of water – the rest can come from water rich foods like vegetables and fruit.

Do your most important job first each day.

It seems so simple but hardly anyone does it! But doing this one thing will make you so much more effective.

There's an interesting story about this. In the 1930s the steel magnate Charles Schwabb had a meeting with a young entrepreneur. This young man offered to teach Schwabb a way to increase his entire company's productivity. All he asked in return was that Schwabb pay him what he thought it was worth.

The idea? Just write down the six most important things you should do each day and do number one first, before going on to number two. After trying this incredibly basic technique for a few weeks Schwabb sent the young man a cheque for $25,000.

Put health before work and you'll be more successful.

Most people in business put health last. By devoting all their time to work they get ahead faster at first, but after a decade or so their body begins to rebel against all the strain, and sickness and mental lethargy slowly build up.

By the time the average person hits 50, they've lost most of their energy and their motivation. The very few people who put their health as their number one priority not only have much more spark in the second half of their careers, they also enjoy their first half a lot more because, being healthy, they're much less prone to stress.

Listen to classical music, not modern.

Much research has been done on how a lot of rock music agitates the human nervous system. You may perhaps have heard of the research test where scientists played hard rock to plants for hours. The plants actually turned away from the speakers!

When played soothing classical music they turned to face the sound, evidently getting strength from it.

In a recent US research study, it was found that most people performed better in IQ tests after listening to classical music, and Sheila Oestrander, the renowned expert on accelerated learning, says students can remember far more when listening to baroque classical pieces.[1]

Switch from rock to classical and both your body and mind will thank you.

Get a mentor.

Find someone who you really respect in an area and ask them to be your coach. It doesn't have to be business, there may be someone you know who's always happy, or supremely fit, maybe they're great at cooking or tennis. Ask them to help you along in that area and form an ongoing relationship with them that's mutually beneficial.

The funny thing is, the more successful someone is, often the more pleasure they get from coaching others in their art.

Become a specialist, not a generalist.

Decades ago generalists ruled the roost. Their knowledge in many fields gave them the competitive edge. But now most industries are getting so complicated that only when you specialise are you likely to be acknowledged as the best in your field. Better to be a master of one important area than an also-ran in three areas.

Keep meetings under ten minutes.

Impossible? Try it, you'll be amazed at how often you can pull it off. And there are great advantages. A ten-minute time limit on meetings forces people to think about the issues they want to discuss prior to the meeting's commencement.

It also stops people babbling on with irrelevancies.

Thirdly, it forces you to concentrate, and thus the resulting ideas are often better.

Two tips to speed up meetings:

1. Have an agenda presented prior to the meeting, notifying participants of a start *and finish* time.

2. Do the meeting standing up.

Dress like the person above you in the company.

If you look and act like someone more senior than you are, when the time comes for promotional reviews, it's easy for your boss to visualise you in a more senior position. If you dress like a junior, your company's CEO will always see you as one.

Discover the power of deep breathing.

The quality of the oxygen you consume is absolutely crucial to the health of your blood and your brain.

Your brain uses a huge proportion of your oxygen intake, over 20%. If it's not getting good oxygen then your thought processes will be impaired. Likewise if your blood isn't well oxygenated, your energy levels will drop.

Whenever you exercise, consciously take deep breaths, using the lower part of your lungs, not just expanding your chest.

Ten deep breaths, three times a day will energise you to a level that will surprise you.

Get out of the office early and work at home more often.

The average office worker is scared to leave the office. Terrified that the boss might think they're lazy, they stay at their desks even if they have little to do. Eradicate that attitude from this moment onwards.

The only thing that matters is your performance, not how many hours you worked, or where you worked. If your work is done, leave, and give yourself a well earned rest. Perhaps the greatest swimmer in history, Mark Spitz, attributed much of his success to his ability to make the most of his time off *between* swimming events, and truly relax.

Likewise if you work better at home, work often at home. Do what gets results, not just what looks good to the corporate lemmings.

Read five business magazines a month.

I know, I know, they're expensive, but just think about this:

If you read five business magazines a month you'll have read 60 a year, and probably over 6000 pages of business information. Isn't it likely that somewhere in all those pages will be at least 20 to 30 great ideas for your business? Maybe even 10 to 20 superb ideas for a new business as well.

You may think you do not have time to read that much: if so, make time. Reading is vital, virtually all the great leaders do it, it just goes with the job.

If you're not up to date with your industry, and those who lead it, your chances of excelling in that industry are, frankly, minimal.

Write Thank You notes daily.

Ever receive a nice Thank You note? It makes you feel terrific, doesn't it? One of the reasons it does is that we receive such notes so rarely.

Don't be like most people and send them once or twice a year. Send them any chance you get and you'll make a favourable impact on hundreds of people each year. People rarely forget those who take the time to say thank you.

Pat Fallon the head of the hot Minneapolis ad agency, Fallon McGelligott, has got this down to a fine art. He sends out an average of 500 Thank You notes a year!

No wonder his agency is one of the fastest growing in America.

when they zig, you zag

Dominate meetings by asking questions.

This is a very powerful and little known fact. The person who asks the most questions is usually the one in control of the meeting. The simple reason is that the questions have to be answered, and people naturally begin to direct their conversation to the questioner. The questioner thus becomes the focus of the meeting.

Try it, you'll be amazed at how well it works.

Set your watch five minutes early.

It's a tiny thing but it sure can make a significant difference to your life.

First of all it reduces your stress levels. Instead of rushing to make it to meetings, you're far more likely to arrive on time, even if you're delayed a little.

Secondly, it's always notable when someone arrives a few minutes early for a meeting. It implies keenness and good organisational ability – two attributes that are prized by everyone successful in the business world.

when they zig, you zag

Do more than you're paid for.

The world is full of people who only do what their official job entails. This may mean they can leave work earlier but it leads to a life of very mediocre achievement.

If you really want to achieve in your career, you have to do more than you're asked. It seems such an obvious thing to say, but so few people ever do it!

If you work harder than you're asked to, and do more than other people in your office do, it's virtually guaranteed you'll get the pay rises and promotions you desire. But if all you do is your job, do you really deserve a pay rise at all?

Never make casual promises.

'I'll ring you tomorrow.' 'I'll meet you at six o'clock.' 'I'll have that report finished by Friday.'

Little promises like these are made all the time and very often not kept. But even though they seem like minor things, powerful people fulfil their little promises, and I'll tell you why:

They understand that a person's word is crucial to their reputation, and if what they promise they always deliver (no matter how small), word gets around that that person can be trusted. And trustworthiness is a much valued personality trait.

The trick is to promise a lot less, then try to exceed what you promised.

Don't drink tap water.

Drinking pure water is one of the best ways you can improve your general health and well-being.

Why? Because your body is over 85% water!

Drinking tap water, which is often filled with chemicals, will over time adversely affect your entire system (see *Eat To Win*[2]). Right around the world more and more people are purifying their tap water or choosing to drink fresh spring water, and are loving the benefits.

Ask people's opinions often.

There are two reasons why this simple technique is very powerful.

The first and most obvious one is that when you bother to ask people what they think, you often hear angles on things you may not have considered yourself.

The second and perhaps the most important reason is that it makes the people you ask feel respected. One of the great lessons of life is to realise that more than money, business people want respect. (Indeed their acquisition of wealth or material possessions is primarily just to gain more respect from other people.)

Every time you ask somebody's opinion you make them feel they're included, and what they think is worth hearing. In other words, you respect them.

Find out all your friends' and business associates' birthdays.

Even important people often only get a few cards on their birthday. If you can take the time to make a list of clients' birthdays and send them a card each year, you'll be remembered fondly by them for life.

Same with your friends. There's hardly a person in the world who doesn't feel warm inside when they get a nice birthday card with some heartfelt words.

Big shot or small player, young or old, everyone loves to be loved.

Act like you're an expert in your field.

A tactic otherwise known as 'Fake it till you make it!'

In business, indeed in life, people are always looking for people who look like they know what they're doing. In a world of ever increasing complexity, people are craving certainty. One of the ways to get that certainty is to surround yourself with experts.

To be successful, you need to look like you're one of those experts.

Now you may be years from mastering your field, but if you can practise looking, talking, moving and generally behaving like an expert you'll make a lot more progress up the career ladder.

Rest assured, all the greats acted like they had made it, before they actually made it. In fact it often became a self-fulfilling prophecy. As the Hollywood legend Cary Grant once remarked, 'I acted like Cary Grant for so long, I became him.'

Shut your office door.

Everyone in management has heard of the 'open door policy', and most live by it. The theory of the open door policy is that staff can always see you about a problem they may have.

Sounds great. But it rarely works.

The reality is that you're constantly getting interruptions to your own work, and your own productivity plummets.

Switch to the closed door policy. For at least three hours a day keep your door closed. Rarely is anything so urgent that it needs your immediate attention, and you'll get a lot more done in a silent environment.

Don't take vitamins just for your body, take them for your mind.

Millions of people take a vitamin C or a multivitamin each day, and for good reason. Vitamins often improve your body's nutrition level, leading to greater feelings of health and higher disease immunity.

But what most people don't realise is that there is a whole range of supplements that can improve your brain power too.

Gingko biloba, selenium, choline, vitamin B and ginseng have all been shown in independent clinical trials to increase both concentration and memory – two vital assets to anyone's daily life.

Always have an opinion.

Want to get nowhere in your career? Agree with the boss all the time.

Most decent bosses hate sycophantic 'yes' men and women. What they're really after are people with firm beliefs, even if those beliefs differ from theirs. They want leaders, and leaders have the guts to speak their mind, without second-guessing their superiors.

If you don't think you can disagree with your boss without penalty, you should resign today. Because that business is heading for the rocks.

Have a memorable business card.

Ninety percent of company business cards are dead boring. No wonder most people throw them away.

Get a card that's a little different. Not silly, but memorable. Prospective clients will not only be more likely to keep the card, they're also more likely to remember the person who gave it to them.

Don't lie.

The great Persian mystic and renowned psychologist, Dr Javad Nurbakhsh, once said that a condition of good mental health and contentment is that you be who you say you are.

The moment you start lying, you begin to have something to hide, and all sorts of mental weaknesses begin to develop from this inconsistency.

Lying not only weakens your character, but surprisingly often it's ineffective as a tactic, simply because lies often get caught out – thereby considerably damaging the reputation of the liar.

Be one of the minority who always tells the truth. Not only will you feel better about yourself, but people will feel better about you.

When everyone knows a person always tells the truth, what they do say has great power and weight.

Look for wrong assumptions in your industry.

How are breakthroughs made in industry?

Well, in almost all cases, true progress is made when somebody questions a commonly held assumption.

Everyone said you couldn't sell computers by direct mail. Michael Dell challenged that assumption and became a billionaire in his thirties.

People said the telephone was not a practical invention. Alexander Bell challenged that assumption and changed communications forever.

In the seventies everyone thought Adidas had the running shoe market tied up. Phil Knight introduced the 'waffle' sole shoe and shot Nike to the top of the industry.

What about your industry? What is assumed by everybody to be true but is actually false?

The answer to this question can lead to breathtaking wealth and achievement.

To protect yourself from cancer, drink green tea.

Most people in the West prefer Ceylon style tea, but drinking green tea is far healthier.

Indeed one study showed that Japanese who consume 4–6 cups of green tea each day have a significantly lower incidence of liver, pancreatic, breast and skin cancer than people who drink less or no green tea at all. In one part of Japan where green tea drinking is at its highest, lung cancer rates are at their lowest.[3]

Develop your vocabulary.

The ability to communicate powerfully is absolutely crucial to success in today's world and, of course, the basic instruments of communication are words.

So any time spent building a powerful vocabulary is time spent well indeed.

I am constantly amazed at how people are impressed when they hear someone use unusual words. I think very often they mistake an extensive vocabulary for high intelligence! The two don't necessarily go together, of course, but if that's what people think then take advantage of it.

Aim to learn a word a week and soon your vocabulary will be rich, powerful and varied.

Use a face moisturiser even if you're male.

Females happily use moisturisers but most males think they're being effeminate if they even consider one.

Let me tell you why they're important. In business, people often have a prejudice against old people. Senior citizens often report finding it harder to get new jobs and to fit in with younger workmates.

So clearly the longer you can stay looking young the better.

Use a face moisturiser every day for the next 20 years and in your final years of business you'll still look like a player, not some over the hill grandpa or granny.

It may be wrong that people judge by appearances, but they do, so accept it and address it.

Give small gifts often.

When you go somewhere for dinner, give the hosts a small gift. Seeing a good friend? Bring along a little present. Meeting up with your lover? Take along a little flower or trinket.

People remember gifts. They appreciate them, it makes them feel special.

A little gift costs you virtually nothing, but the impact you make can be enormous.

Remember, the people who really get on in this world are the people who can make others feel special.

Always let the boss know what you've done.

The secret of success in a corporation is *not* doing a good job. It's doing a good job *and* making sure your boss knows about it!

Many a middle-ranked executive has failed to make it to the top because they neglected to keep the boss closely informed about all the good things they were up to.

On the other hand, many mediocre workers have been promoted because they constantly let their boss know about their successes.

Get smart, and get communicating. As long as you don't gloat, you are your own best advertisement.

Buy three expensive ties or scarves.

Good ties (and scarves on women) get noticed.

When people see somebody wearing a beautiful tie or scarf, they often assume the rest of their clothes are expensive too. (Even if you got them from Target.)

They also often assume that the tie or scarf wearer is successful, intelligent and stylish.

Now, as we all know, very often none of these things is true! But you'd be mad not to give yourself the advantage of making a good first impression, and a beautiful tie or scarf will do that for almost anyone.

Don't watch TV for more than an hour a week.

The average person is not particularly
successful and the average person watches
four hours of television every day. A
coincidence? I think not.

It's not so much that TV is bad in itself,
rather that you can do so many more
productive things with the same hours – read,
meet people, work on your goals, exercise,
dream . . . basically live life to the full.

There is no greater time waster than the
television, and when you lose your time you
lose your life.

Reward yourself every single day.

Most people give up before they achieve their goals. This would happen far less if people gave themselves little rewards along the way. Giving yourself a little gift, like dinner at a nice restaurant, a new shirt or a weekend away if you finish a major task, makes working much more inspiring and fun.

If the only reward you get comes at the end of the goal it makes the journey much harder.

Develop a strong self image.

The vast majority of people do no work on developing a healthy self image. Indeed many people see themselves generally as failures at life.

In his classic book *Psycho Cybernetics*, Dr Maxwell Maltz[4] clearly showed that our self image usually dictates our level of success.

Each time you look in the mirror, affirm to yourself that you *are* talented, and *do* deserve success. Take control of your self image from this moment onwards, and reap the benefits for the rest of your life.

Spend half an hour a day thinking.

That's right, just thinking.

Sadly, most people do virtually no quality thinking in a year let alone a day.

As Henry Ford said, 'Thinking is the hardest work there is, which is probably why so few engage in it.'

Most fortunes start with a great idea, and a lot of hard work. Most people have got the hard work bit right, they just didn't spend long enough thinking of the right idea.

The founder of IBM, Thomas Watson, had signs put up around his company that said just one word: 'Think'!!!

Eliminate clutter in the office.

Clean desks lead to clear minds. Get rid of 90% of the paper that lands on your desk. Either give it to someone else or bin it.

I once read an article in *Success* magazine about a guy who charged $1000 to teach people how to maintain a neat desk. One of his main methods was to change the question in your mind from, 'Will I need this again?' to 'Can I get a copy of this again if I need it?'. When I took his advice my desk immediately became 50% cleaner.

By the way, the great super computer designer, Seymour Cray, worked with nothing on his desk but a pad of geometrically lined paper and a pen, so critical did he believe a clean desk was to clear thinking.

Guard your mind.

Most people are victims to the vagaries of
circumstance. When things are going great
they're happy. When things are lousy, they
turn miserable. Up and down their moods go,
almost totally dependent on outside
conditions.

Real champions are different. They guard
their minds so that even when things are
going poorly they stay calm, relaxed, happy
and, most importantly, hopeful. The ability to
stay positive and always expect the best is
crucial to success.

Here's what perhaps the greatest
bodybuilder of all time, Arnold
Schwarzenegger, said about the matter: 'A
positive attitude and confidence in your
ability are absolutely necessary to make your
best gains. . . . Whether it's building a Mr
Olympia physique, climbing a mountain,
succeeding in business, getting an
educational degree, or learning to play a
musical instrument, everything starts with the
mind. You have to do it first in your mind
and believe you can do it in your heart.'[5]

Never underestimate the power of a smile.

The power of a sincere smile is incredible!

Here's three ways smiling can change your life:

1. A sincere smile makes others feel good. A fantastic grin can lift almost anyone's spirits, and singlehandedly change the mood of a room.

2. A smile says you're confident, that you're on top of things. It says you're in control.

3. It's a clinically proven fact that a big smile stimulates the thymus gland located below your throat, which then produces pleasure-increasing opiates. So when you smile, you'll actually begin to feel happier inside.

Reply to letters on the same paper they are written on.

This is a great time saving tip recommended by time management guru, Alan Lakein.[6]

Think about it. Replying on the same letter saves you typing it, and saves paper. It also lets you hand write, making your reply seem more personal.

Because the sender receives his or her own letter back you often have to write less too, as he or she is reminded of the questions they asked by seeing their own letter again.

I've been using this technique for five years now and I estimate it has reduced the time taken to reply to letters by half.

Aim to be the best in the world at what you do.

Am I crazy? What are the chances of you ever being the best in the world at something? Pretty darn small. But unless you aim for greatness, you never achieve above mediocrity.

Always be thinking, 'What would the best in the world do in this situation?', and you'll be amazed at the progress you make.

Forget where you are now, *keep thinking about where you'd like to be*. Strange as it may seem, if you aim sincerely to be the number one in the world at something, many seemingly unrelated areas of your life will also improve.

Don't listen to music in the car, listen to educational tapes.

The average person spends tens of hours every week in the car. In fact, it's estimated that typically many of us spend two weeks a year just driving!

Don't waste that time. Learn a language, get inspired, hear a lecture from an expert in your field – all via audio cassettes available at your local bookstore.

These days virtually any bookstore has a wide selection of tapes that can enhance your life in numerous areas. Pick some that interest you and create your own mobile university!

Plan your holidays at the beginning of the year.

It's a strange thing, but a holiday starts when you book it. Indeed, some of the best parts of a holiday are the months of anticipation leading up to it – reading the brochure, planning where you want to go, getting advice and hearing the experiences of friends who've been there, etc . . .

However, many people decide on a holiday just a month or two before they go on it, thereby forfeiting that joy of anticipation. (When you know you've got a holiday coming up, it makes working those long hours a lot more bearable too.)

Book a holiday this week and you will immediately feel better about your life.

You may have to cancel, but after months of fun daydreaming about it, I bet you don't.

Don't socialise too much.

While it's always good to hang out with friends, be careful not to do it to excess.

Get too busy socialising and you'll find you simply don't have the time, or the energy, to achieve anything worthwhile.

In today's society, regular socialising often means regular alcohol consumption, a habit that can lead not only to decreased general motivation, but a weakened metabolism as well.

I'm not suggesting becoming a monk, but rather a balance between after-hours' action and rest.

Life is short. Spend too much time partying and you'll find your life has passed before you've achieved anything worthwhile.

Always ask for more money than you want.

It's new job time. You're at the interview, and your interviewer gets down to money. How much do you want?

Never tell them. Always ask for 10% more than you want. The reasons are simple. Firstly, they may say yes to your first amount, in which case you've just paid for your overseas holiday this year.

Secondly, most business people can't resist trying to get a bargain. Seven times out of ten they'll try to lower your asking price, so you have to allow for that.

Another key point: Always summarise why you're going to do a fantastic job for that company in the same breath as you mention your salary – it helps remind them you're worth every cent of what you're asking for.

Follow the rules of Feng Shui.

Feng Shui is the ancient art of balancing energy flow in your home and workplace to create harmony and good luck.

It may sound like mumbo jumbo, but millions of Asians believe that the placement of furniture and the design of buildings can influence good fortune. You may scoff at this, but you should know that some of the world's richest men (indeed most of Hong Kong's billionaires) swear by it.

Check out your local bookstores for books on Feng Shui.[7]

Have the shiniest shoes in the office.

Few people worry about them, but superbly shined shoes can make a real impression. Immaculately kept footwear says a lot about a person.

It says:

1. They care about their personal presentation.

2. They are concerned about details.

3. They're organised enough to have time to polish their shoes.

4. They have personal pride.

Are these attributes of successful people? You bet.

But there's another benefit to well maintained footwear. You feel great wearing superbly presented shoes, and when you feel great, you usually perform well too.

Make decisions often.

Most people take too long to make decisions, and then change their mind often.

Successful people do the opposite.

They tend to study the pros and cons of a situation, then decide quickly.

There's an old saying about this matter, 'You don't have as many problems as you have decisions to make.' I think you'll find it's true. Make the decision and life usually becomes so much simpler. Fail to make it, and there's always uncertainty and lack of commitment.

Kevin Roberts, the chief executive of one of the world's biggest advertising agencies, Saatchi and Saatchi, is famous for making fast decisions. 'I figure that even if a few of them are wrong, I'll have made more progress than if I'd done nothing.'

Heed that wisdom.

Throw out half of
what you own.

Half the clothes you own you rarely wear.
Half the possessions you have you either
never use or place little value on.

Make the decision to keep only what's
beautiful or really useful.

It may seem a radical thing to do, but the
rewards are significant. You'll have a cleaner
environment, your dry cleaning bills will be
lower, you'll be able to find things more
easily, and you'll value what you've got left
much more.

And if you give it all to the poor, you'll
also feel really good inside.

Keep a 'Things Achieved' list.

Ever think you're making no progress in your life? Create a 'Things Achieved' journal.

At the end of each day, write in it what you achieved – the big things and the little things, in your business life and your personal domain.

It's a great way to feel better about your life, because inevitably you realise that you're achieving far more than you expected. Plus having the journal on your desk makes you very achievement-orientated, knowing that you have to fill it.

Be constantly upbeat in the office.

People love being around positive, uplifting people. Their vibrant energy gets everybody around them charged up and feeling good. Likewise, people tend to steer clear of a miserable moper.

Make the decision now to force yourself to act happy (even when you don't feel happy), and your success with people will significantly improve.

Remember, happiness is just a choice, it doesn't have to be a good day or a lousy one. You can choose to be happy even if you're having a disastrous time, you really can. If you do, you'll not only be more liked by people, you'll feel better about life in general.

Learn how to come up with ideas.

Take it from somebody who's made their whole career out of conceiving good ideas, creativity is not just something you're born with, you *can* develop it. The trick is to learn some creativity techniques. Here are two quick ones:

Dictionary method: Open a dictionary and pick a simple word out of it. Then relate your particular problem to that word. What ideas does that word give you? You'll be amazed at the results.

What would my competitor do?: Pretend you're the competition. If they were running your company, what decisions would they make? What directions would they go?

With elementary techniques such as these you can become a veritable fountain of ideas.[8]

Take ten risks each year.

Most people play it safe.

As one writer put it, they tip-toe through life hoping to make it safely to death! How absurd is that!

Think about five successes you have had in your life. Isn't it true that most of them came about because you took a risk? **Regular risk is the key to success.** As long as it is carried out carefully and rationally.

Get a piece of paper, number 1–10 on it and stick it on a wall in your bathroom. At the top of it write 'Risks I have taken lately'. Make sure that by the end of the year it is full. Only when you are not afraid of risk can you expect uncommon levels of success.

The reality of life is that, in truth, playing it safe is the riskiest thing that you can do.

Don't drink from aluminium cans.

The jury is still out, but there is research that suggests eating or drinking from aluminium could be dangerous.

Researchers have found that people suffering memory loss showed above average levels of aluminium in their blood. The three regions of the world with the most aluminium in their soil also have a high incidence of Parkinson's disease. Significant levels of aluminium were discovered to accumulate in the brain of many people with Alzheimer's disease.[9]

Despite this research, it must be stressed that aluminium's dangers are still not proven, but obviously it's better to be safe than sorry. Don't use aluminium cooking utensils (they're already banned in four European countries) and don't drink liquids from aluminium containers.

Constantly give.

I believe there is a law of the universe that when acted upon gives you 100% certain success. That law is 'You get back what you give'.

I believe this law is so fundamental to how the world works that ignoring it dooms one to failure, no matter what field of endeavour one is involved in.

But millions of people expect to get rich without effort, to succeed with ease, a result as impossible as the farmer who attempts to reap a great harvest without planting seeds and watering them.

If you want love give it, if you want wealth help others to make money or improve their life, if you wish to be happy then work on spreading happiness daily.

By changing your habitual question from 'What can I get?' to 'What can I contribute?', virtually every aspect of your life will change for the better, within one month.

Keep memos and reports to one page and insist others do the same.

Brevity forces clarity.

The Everything On One Page rule encourages people to think more about what they're writing, and eradicates fuzzy thinking. It reduces paper in your office or home dramatically, and streamlines the communication process.

Now you probably think that your issues are far too important to be summarised in one page. Let me just remind you that no less a leader than Winston Churchill once asked for a complete summary of the Royal Navy's preparedness for war – but insisted that that report be just one page long.

Look after your relatives.

As people get older, they tend to move away from regular contact with family and relatives.

This is often a great mistake, because these people come from similar backgrounds, and so still have much to offer you.

More importantly, the old saying 'Blood is thicker than water' tends to be true. Like them or not, it's your relatives who often come to your rescue when many of your so-called 'friends' have abandoned you.

Never buy a new car.

Buy one six months to a year old.

The moment you drive a new car out of the showroom, its value usually depreciates by 20%. Now *that's* a bad investment.

Buy a car that's only six months old, however, and it still feels new but is much, much better value. Not only do you buy it cheaper, you'll lose less on it when you sell it, as much of its depreciation occurred before you purchased it.

Don't go to university unless you have to.

Some of the most successful people in the world never had a university degree. So don't be fooled by those who say you can't be successful without formal education. It's hogwash.

Apple Computer founder, Steve Jobs, never got a degree. Stephen Spielberg's training was purely on the job. Billionaire music mogul David Geffen started out in a company mailroom. Their success depended on their own effort and tenacity, not on years of academic training.

Having said that, let me emphasise that I have nothing against degrees. Indeed, for many careers they're not only helpful, they're absolutely essential.

All I'm saying is, don't go to university just because you think it's the right thing to do. Go if you think you'll enjoy it or if it's crucial to your career progress, but never go because of social convention or peer group pressure.

Life's too short to be doing things that you're not really committed to.

Always put your watch and wallet in the same place.

There are few things more stressful than being late for an appointment and not being able to find your keys or wallet.

Believe me, I know. I've come close to missing planes countless times searching my entire home for them. Finally I wised up, and committed to putting them in the same place (on my bedroom shelf) every time. It works.

But keys and money are just the start. Think of the ten things you use most often, and commit now to creating a special, easy to find place for them.

Your life will be considerably less stressful if you do . . .

Associate with the kind of people you want to become.

If you want to be a great musician, hang out with great musicians. If you'd like to be an excellent mother, associate with terrific mothers. If business is your thing, you'll profit greatly by socialising with good business people.

Remember, you become like the people you associate with, and as the saying goes, 'If you lie down with dogs, you'll get up with fleas.'

Take a good look at the people you spend the most time with. Do they lift you up or bring you down? Do they inspire you or do you have to do all the inspiring? Are they quality people or riff-raff?

Be careful who you associate with. Your friends can affect your life more than you may realise.

Don't take more than 20 minutes off for lunch.

Big lunch breaks get you out of the mood for work. Quite often you'll return from lunch sluggish and not in the mood to perform at a peak level. A 20 minute lunch is long enough to provide a relaxing break, but short enough that you won't slip out of work mode.

Eat brainfoods.

Most people eat for taste, but the right diet can actually help you think better. Dr William Vayda, author of *Psycho Nutrition*[10] suggests eating a little pasta if you wish to relax (it encourages a release of the feel-good chemical, serotonin, in you) and foods high in protein if you need to concentrate in the next few hours. Nuts, egg and potato are also said by Dr Vayda to be excellent for enhancing thinking.

Work and sleep with a negative ion generator nearby.

The quality of your health and your mind's ability to think is greatly affected by the air you breathe.

Poor quality oxygen will make you feel sluggish physically and mentally. Purify the air you breathe! Buy a negative ion generator from your local department store and you'll be amazed at how much more invigorated you feel.

Negative ion generators, as the name suggests, pump millions of negative ions into your environment. These ions help balance and purify the air, which in cities is usually dominated by positive ions.

You'll have more energy and you'll be able to concentrate for longer – priceless assets in today's high pressure world.

Make your home a mind gym.

Recently experts on the human brain discovered a remarkable thing. Contrary to popular opinion, you do not have to get more senile as you get older (see *Brain Longevity*).[11]

On the contrary, extensive research has revealed that if you keep using your brain you can actually get brighter and brighter as years go by!

Here's a few tips for keeping your brain sharp:

- Play chess or draughts a few days a week.
- Play along with the quiz shows on TV.
- Read at least half an hour each day.
- Invite different people over for dinner.
- Cook something unusual twice a week.
- Write letters to people you're rarely in contact with.
- Learn a language at home.
- Play charades occasionally.
- Rearrange the furniture.

They're only little things, but they help keep your brain active and healthy, turning a home into a gymnasium for the brain.

Schedule all meetings in the afternoon.

The fact is minds tend to be fresher in the morning. That's why it's by far the best time to get your hardest mental work done. Most people accept this, and yet still fill that priceless morning thinking period up with dull, often unimportant meetings.

What a waste!

Schedule your meetings for the afternoon, when most people have mentally slowed down for the day. Then at least you can make your mornings truly productive, and will have the satisfaction of achieving some major tasks even before lunchtime.

Don't work under fluorescent lights.

A US study in 1983 showed that you're twice as likely to get skin cancer if you work or live under fluorescent lights.

A Canadian study in 1992 also showed that fluorescent lighting can lead to an increased risk of melanoma.[12]

Why risk it? Replace your fluorescent lights with bulbs.

Drink less alcohol.

A glass of wine a day helps you relax, and may even prolong your life. But regular alcohol consumption above that can do tremendous harm.

According to Dr William Vayda, the president of the International College of Applied Nutrition,[13] excess alcohol use can lead to:

- Increased anxiety
- Imbalanced sex hormones
- Increased fat deposits
- A slowdown in the body's repair mechanisms
- Abnormal ratios of important brain chemicals
- A weakening of the heart muscle
- Higher blood pressure
- Lots of other nasty side effects.

Drink less alcohol than the average person and you'll be a lot healthier and happier than the average person.

Reduce PMT by changing your diet.

More than half the female population of Australia suffers from premenstrual tension.

You don't have to be one of them. Change your diet and you'll almost certainly relieve it.

How? Well, excessive consumption of alcohol and eating lots of sugary foods and refined carbohydrates help contribute to PMT. Reduce them.

Taking vitamin B6, zinc, magnesium, ascorbic acid tablets and more proteins should help too.

A tablet of spirulina (used by the Aztecs thousands of years ago) will also do wonders if you're unlucky enough to suffer from this emotionally draining problem.

when they zig, you zag

Give to every charity that asks.

The reasons are simple.

One, you always feel great when you give money to the needy. Why not feel great more often?

Two, each time you give to charity it reminds you how lucky you are, and makes all your problems look pretty petty in comparison to truly poor or disadvantaged people.

Three, regularly giving money away helps you to become less attached to it. The obsession with acquiring money is a desire that can never be satisfied. Anything you can do to weaken that impulse is definitely good for your character.

Use the power of aromatherapy.

Aromatherapy is a proven mood changer. The subtle smells are picked up by the limbic system in the brain, the most primitive and one of its most powerful parts.

There's an essential oil that can get you into almost any mood you choose.

For increased relaxation use lavender in your bath.

For increased romantic feelings, put ylang ylang in an oil burner.

Basil, lemon or orange can increase concentration and geranium can make you feel more positive.

Using aromatherapy at home or in your office will do wonders for your well-being, mentally, physically and spiritually.

Get up no later than 6.00a.m.

Stick to this even if it means you're a little short of sleep (you can always catch up with a big snooze on weekends).

An early start makes you feel great the rest of the day. You feel on top of things. It also allows you enough time to do numerous life-enhancing tasks, like exercise, reading your goals, planning the day, spending unrushed time with loved ones, etc.

Indian Ayurvedic doctors believe getting up earlier regularly makes you healthier too, as the air you breathe is fresher and more energised.

The advantages far outweigh the disadvantages.

Have a spiritual life.

There are two big reasons why you should try to get to know God, and follow a religion.

The first is that nobody really knows whether there is a God or not – there's a 50% chance either way. Those being the odds, though, it makes no sense at all to bet all your money on there being no God, and possibly deeply regretting that bet in the afterlife!

If there's at least an equal chance that there is a God, then you'd be mad not to investigate the spiritual areas, study them, become an expert on them, and live them to the full. That way you'll be fully equipped to handle whatever the future holds. After all, you'll be dead a long time.

The other reason why living a spiritual life makes sense is purely scientific. Numerous tests on religious people have found that they generally have lower stress, lower heart rates, less cholesterol and lead happier lives than people who don't practise a faith.[14]

So it seems that living spiritually doesn't just help you in the next life, but in this one as well.

when they zig, you zag

Read every major book in your field.

Albert Einstein said that anyone could become an expert in their field. All they had to do is read a book on that subject for one hour a day . . . for the rest of their life.

He's right, of course. But that daily study is much more effort than most people are prepared to put in. What a shame, because it's precisely that extra knowledge that makes the difference between a mediocre practitioner and a master.

By reading every important book in your field you equip yourself with the thoughts and strategies of the kings of your profession.

Some of it has to rub off onto you.

Plan your recreation.

People have no problem planning their workday, but often throw such planning out the window when it comes to their time off.

This is madness, as in many ways our recreation is more important than our occupation. It's time we can use to improve relationships, get healthy, de-stress and generally enjoy life. It should definitely not be wasted.

Before you go home at night, or prior to a weekend, spend a couple of minutes working out how you can make the most of your leisure time. That way when you do return to work, you'll arrive refreshed and invigorated, not still stressed and irritated.

when they zig, you zag

Get 20 minutes sun each day.

In Australia the majority of the population looks at the sun in two ways.

They either love it, and end up spending too long in it and get aged by its powerful rays. Or they hate it, and never get exposed to its beneficial effects.

Modern research suggests both lifestyles are wrong. While everyone knows too much sun is harmful, few people are aware that too little sun is harmful too.

The solution, as always, is neither extreme. Twenty minutes sunlight a day provides the body with a vital source of vitamin D. Get 20 minutes daily and you'll be far healthier than if you avoid sunlight altogether.

Best times are morning or late afternoon, but never at lunchtime.

when they zig, you zag

Always ask 'What will my industry look like ten years from now?'

Most people are so caught up with their day-to-day problems that they rarely look deeply into the future. (If they did they probably wouldn't have so many day-to-day problems in the first place.)

I remember once asking Michael Dell, at 32 definitely one of the youngest billionaires in the world, how much time he spent envisioning the future for Dell Computers. He told me fully one-third of his time was devoted to looking far out beyond the horizon.

If a man as busy as Michael Dell can find the time to spend a third of his working hours future-gazing, then we can too.

Never have a holiday at home.

It may be cheap, but it's rarely relaxing.

When you stay at home during your holiday you tend to just mope around and clean up the house. It's not particularly enjoyable, and it's certainly not refreshing for the mind.

A change of environment is vital to getting a good break. When you go somewhere new, even if it's just a country shack a few hours' drive away, you forget about life back home. You experience new things and break your usual mental habits, your brain and soul get a wake up call.

Time changes too. One week in a different environment often makes you feel like you've taken three weeks off, whereas time at home goes by in a flash.

Get rid of addictions.

Drugs. Alcohol. Cigarettes. Food. Television. Gossiping. Jealousy. Selfish behaviour . . . What are your addictions?

We all have them, and each one chains us to mediocrity. If you really want freedom, if you really desire happiness, then go to work on eradicating anything that you are a slave to. Inch by inch, bit by bit, you can resist your addictions, until finally you break them completely.

And with each one you do break, your life will move to a new level of joy . . .

Exercise daily.

Something. Anything! But do it daily.

The body was made to move! Depriving your body of daily rigorous movement is unnatural and devastating to psychological health.

Countless studies show that people who don't exercise regularly are more stressed, less happy and even less intelligent.

And if your excuse is you don't have the time, don't kid yourself. If President Clinton can find time for a morning jog, with all the pressures of his nation (and indeed the world) on his shoulders, then so can you.

Avoid business partnerships.

There's an old saying, 'The only ship that's certain to sink is a partnership.'

There's a lot of truth to that. A business partnership is like a marriage, except that you usually spend more time with your business partner than your spouse.

All this time together means pretty soon you get sick of each other and start arguing about ever more trivial issues. I'm not saying this is always the case, but it's often the case (which is one of the reasons four out of five businesses eventually fail).

If you can, own your business outright, or at least be the majority shareholder. Yes, it's a lot more work, but it's usually a lot less stressful politically too.

I've been in business around 15 years, and it's only in the last year that I've found a business partner I'm comfortable with.

Until you're absolutely sure you've got a great partner lined up, sail the ship yourself.

when they zig, you zag

Read the five great success books.

There are many great books on the art and science of success, and which are the best is a highly subjective area.

But the five books I mention here are my personal favourites and have inspired hundreds of millions of people to pick themselves up and create brilliant lives.

1. **The Bible.** Even if you're not religious, this book has such deep wisdom, it can uplift and transform you.

2. **Think And Grow Rich.** Napoleon Hill spent over 20 years meeting and studying the most successful men in America. Then wrote about their common modes of thought and action.

3. **The Seven Habits Of Highly Effective People.** Stephen Covey's masterpiece. Written in the 1980s it has helped turn the Covey Leadership Center into a $500 million annual turnover business.

4. **The Road Less Travelled.** Over five years in the *New York Times* best seller lists. Scott M. Peck's book emphasises that there are no easy ways to success and happiness, but that both are possible when one works on one's own personal integrity.

5. **Unlimited Power.** When Anthony Robbins wrote this he was still in his twenties. But for an aggressive approach to sculpting yourself into the person of your dreams, it's hard to beat.

Any one of these books has the power to transform your life. Read all of them (and put them into practice) and I cannot imagine you not living an absolutely magnificent life.

Eat mainly vegetables and fruit.

A crucial ingredient to success and happiness is energy. Without a strong supply of energy to propel you through the day, your mood will drop and lethargy will set in. With this in mind, it pays to keep your diet healthy and light.

Vegetables and fruit are definitely light, in fact they're usually over 80% water! They're also low in fat, and having a low fat diet is a proven method of keeping the brain healthy in old age, according to Alzheimer's expert Dr Dharma Singh Khalsa.[15]

And remember this: Digesting food is the second biggest user of the body's energy supply (after sex). So if you're always eating heavy foods, like meat, your body will always be using a huge amount of energy just to process your meals, often leaving you tired and listless at the end of each day.

Most Westerners have a 50% meat diet, at least. Get it down to 20–30% and you'll really notice a boost in energy levels.

Never exercise hard.

According to Dr Kenneth Cooper, the man who invented the term 'Aerobics', intense physical exercise actually decreases your chances of being healthy.

The stress of heavy physical exertion causes the body to produce 'free radicals', unbalanced cells that can actually weaken your body's disease-defence system.

According to Cooper, light exercise is the way to go, along with regular consumption of antioxidants – vitamins B, C, and betacarotene for example.

Don't spend too much time alone.

Research indicates that people who spend lots of time alone tend to have lower levels of happiness.

Maybe it's because when you're by yourself you think too much, or maybe it's because you don't get to express yourself to others, we can only guess.

Don't get me wrong. In many ways I myself am a loner, I certainly enjoy getting away from the madding crowd. But too much isolation can definitely be damaging to the psyche . . .

Constantly think about your profession.

Failures work in their business. Successes work *on* their business – creating systems, thinking about the future, clarifying responsibilities, etc . . .

Let me be frank. You can't create something big and special unless you're constantly giving it thought, night and day.

If you're not prepared to devote yourself to that kind of quality thinking time then sooner or later you'll be overtaken by a competitor who is.

Remember, I'm not suggesting you *work* night and day, but *think* night and day. The difference between the two when it comes to results is enormous.

Study Neuro Linguistic Programming.

NLP is one of the most important breakthroughs in human performance in the last century. Developed by Messrs Grindler and Bandler in the early 1970s, it's a series of techniques designed to enable anyone to achieve mastery in their field, by improving their mental functioning.

Let me briefly explain one NLP technique, known as the Swoosh pattern.

Think of something you hate doing – the gardening, for instance. Now think of something you love . . . perhaps it's chocolate cake.

Right, now see a picture in your mind of yourself doing the gardening. Then while loudly saying the word, 'Swoosh!' replace that gardening picture with a picture of chocolate cake. Slide the new picture on from the right until it has quickly replaced the old scene of you gardening.

By simply doing this 20 or so times in a row, believe it or not, your brain will actually begin to mix the two feelings and will soon like to do the gardening much more!

It sounds bizarre but it works.

But that's just one of a series of NLP techniques that can help improve your life. There are numerous books on NLP in all major bookstores so do yourself a favour and check them out.

Take holidays often.

I've met so many people working in companies that never take their annual holidays. They say they're too busy.

What a load of garbage. If you honestly can't find the time to take a decent break, then your business is simply too disorganised. And in actual fact, you're not doing your company a service at all by not having a holiday.

A good holiday freshens the mind and the body. People who don't take breaks are often stale thinkers, and are usually too stressed to contribute anything brilliant anyway.

Finally, I believe you get many of your best ideas when you're on holiday. Your mind thinks big thoughts, away from the constant grind of urgent deadlines.

Get out of the office, and go on holiday. Not only will you think better, you'll be much more pleasant to be around.

Schedule time to do nothing. Often.

Our world is too busy.

This busyness has created a population where stress-related heart disease and cancer is at an all time high.

Get off the treadmill. Make the effort to schedule at least a few minutes a day where you can do absolutely nothing.

At first you'll feel guilty doing nothing (which shows you how sick our society has become). But after a while your mind and body will really look forward to these peaceful times, and when you eventually return into the hustle and bustle of the world, you'll do so refreshed and renewed.

Aim to triple what you earn, not increase it by $20,000.

One of the fundamental differences between hugely successful people and also-rans is how high they aim.

If you set out to triple your income in a year you may not make it, but you'll sure earn a lot more than if you aimed for a 'sensible' increase. Small goals aren't motivating, they lack the excitement factor. Aim high and you instantly set yourself apart from 95% of society.

As the great advertising writer Leo Burnett once said, 'Reach for the stars. You may not grab them, but you won't end up with a handful of mud either.'

Visualise daily.

Spend five minutes a day seeing a 'movie' in
your mind of how you'd like your life to be.
The brain is 88% subconscious, and the
subconscious cannot tell the difference
between an event vividly visualised and one
that has actually happened. Therefore if you
consistently 'see' yourself performing a
certain way, you'll begin to perform at that
level in real life.

Ask any gold medal Olympian,
visualisation works. The fact that most people
in business don't visualise opens up a
treasure chest of opportunities for you.

Write your 'To Do' list the night before.

These days most intelligent people create a daily 'To Do' list. But many of them write theirs once they've arrived at work.

There are two problems with this. Firstly, you're often writing it under pressure, already being hounded by workmates and deadlines. Secondly, you don't feel nearly as organised and on top of things as if you do it in the peace and quiet of your study or bedroom at home the evening before. 'To Do' lists are important. Maximise their effectiveness by getting them done early and properly.

Read biographies.

Most people read fiction, if they read books at all. (In fact only 10% of Australians even read one book a year.) You're much better off reading biographies or autobiographies of great leaders, business people, saints and sporting heroes.

By reading about society's champions you'll be far more inspired to become one yourself.

Hangovers are easy to relieve.

You don't have to live for hours with a hangover!

Here are five scientifically proven ways to decrease the effects of a big night on the town.

1. Take B-complex vitamins and vitamin C. A good dose of vitamin C helps absorb the alcohol and assists the liver to break it down.

2. Evening primrose oil is excellent, according to US research.

3. Drink fruit juices.

4. Drink lots of fluids before and after your binge.

5. Stay up for an extra couple of hours after drinking.

Hire slow, sack fast.

Most executives do the opposite. They choose their staff quickly, without checking references, having multiple interviews, or evaluating all possible candidates. Then when they discover they've hired a dud, they don't have the heart to get rid of them.

Successful executives never rush into hiring staff. But if they do have a poor performer, they give them some coaching, some warnings, then if they're still mediocre they ditch them pronto.

The health of the overall company is just too important to let mediocre minds bring it down.

And don't feel too bad about the ones you let go. If they're any good, the sacking will be just the wake-up call they need to lift their game and get back onto the road to success.

Train yourself to expect the best.

When you expect good things to happen and goals to be achieved, you work more confidently and often get more done.

Doctor Martin Seligman, author of *Learned Optimism*,[16] says positive thinkers are not only healthier and happier, but also more successful. But it takes discipline. Train yourself to replace every thought of failure with an expectation of success and your entire life will soon change for the better.

Delegate everything possible.

Most people spend far too much of their day doing unimportant things.

Delegate the laundry! Delegate the car washing! Delegate the house cleaning! Then spend the hours you save doing things that will really enrich your career and your home life.

Most people think they can't afford to get hired help for these irksome tasks. But as the renowned high performance expert, Dr Frederick Grosse, pointed out, with all the time you'd save you could make a heck of a lot more money.[17]

Think about it. It makes tremendous sense.

Always push yourself.

There's never been a champion in any field who didn't develop the habit of pushing themselves to succeed just that little bit more in their profession.

These days the difference between winning an Olympic Gold Medal and coming fifth is often a fraction of a second. The difference between winning a business contract and being runner up is often just as small. Perfect the little things, finesse the flaws and inch by inch you'll move ahead of the pack. If 'good enough' is good enough, you'll never be good enough to be great.

Use natural tranquillisers.

Many people needing to relax look to drugs or alcohol.

But there's a whole range of natural tranquillisers that can relax you without those side effects.

For instance zinc calms the nerves. (You'll find tuna, veal, lamb, milk, bran, mushrooms and beef high in zinc.)

Vitamin C is a brilliant mind relaxant, but large doses are necessary.

And many of the B vitamins can help emotional disorders, particularly B12. It's available in tablets or in egg yolk, yoghurt, chicken, cheese, prunes, shellfish, pork and milk.

Don't work hard, work carefully.

Hard work does not make you rich. The world is full of people who work 70 hours a week and still aren't wealthy. The big money comes when you work carefully, only spending time doing things that actually increase your company's income, instead of wasting hours every day chatting, eating, on the phone or in meetings. Most people work less than 15 income-producing hours a week.

Don't work just for the money. You'll end up with less money.

You'll rarely meet a millionaire who doesn't love his or her work. When you love what you do, you work with greater enthusiasm, passion and commitment. If you take a job you don't like just for the money, within months your work becomes sluggish and ill-disciplined. Within a few years you'll be overtaken on the career ladder by those people who just did what they loved, and got stuck right into it.

Eat less meat to stay healthier.

German researchers at the Cancer Research Centre studied 1904 vegetarians for five years. They were amazed to see that these vegetarians had only 37% of the number of deaths of the average meat eating population.

In Britain researchers observed 4671 vegetarians for a full seven years. Their death rate was just half that of the general population.

I'm not suggesting you give up meat entirely, but halving the amount of meat you eat now is probably a great way to increase your chances of staying alive.

Don't go into industries on the upswing. There's usually too much competition.

In every boom market, scores of school graduates want to get into stockbroking or real estate. In every bust cycle nobody does. Except the smart ones. You see, when you enter an industry that's temporarily unpopular, there are more good jobs available and less competition. Also, when a boom period finally does come around (everything is cyclical) you'll be a senior employee not a junior one, and so will be in a far better position to take advantage of it.

Be part of the 3% who write down life goals.

Here's a fascinating study.

In 1952 some researchers interviewed the graduates of Yale University, one of the USA's premier Ivy League universities.[18]

Amongst many other questions, they asked each of them whether they had a written goals plan for their life.

Ninety-seven percent didn't.

However, 20 years later, the researchers returned to interview the surviving members of that class. Incredibly, they found that the 3% who did write down their goals not only reported better all round life satisfaction, *they also earned more than the 97% who didn't put it together.*

Write down your goals, and read them daily. As the great human potential expert Brian Tracey once said, 'I know of very few poor people with goals and very few rich people without them.'

Don't wear sunglasses all the time.

It may look cool, but it's not good for your eyes.

The eye's retina needs light. In fact, if it is denied large doses of natural light it will begin to get weaker.

A person who wears sunglasses all day for a decade will have considerably weaker eyes than someone who only wears them when the sun is bright.

Sunglasses are beneficial, but just not all the time.

Do all trivial administration at the end of the week.

If your life is like mine, you probably get numerous phone calls and a mountain of mail every day.

If you respond to that as soon as you get it, then you're just letting other people run your life.

If it's not important, leave it till Friday afternoon at 5 o'clock, then handle it all in one hour.

That way your week will have a lot fewer trivial interruptions and you'll end up having achieved a lot more.

Model successful people.

There are two major ways to reach the top of your chosen field.

The first is to learn by your own experience. This works well but can be very slow, and can lead to making a lot of mistakes.

The second is to model people who are already at the top of your field. Take them to lunch, read about them, study their work habits and thinking – then emulate them.

Copying the success strategies of people who are at the top is quick and effective. In fact few people ever make it to the top without choosing the second route.

Steal ideas from other industries and areas.

The invention of Liquid Paper® made a huge impact in offices in the 1970s. But its concept of 'whiting out' mistakes is what the painting industry had been doing for centuries.

The creation of Velcro™ revolutionised the clothing industry practically overnight. But its inventor says he got the idea from noticing how burrs from plants stuck to his legs as he walked by.

Many of the most brilliant breakthroughs in industry occur when there is a cross-fertilisation of concepts from two different areas.

When looking to advance your business, don't just look at the competitors. Look at many fields and ask yourself, 'Would these concepts work in our industry?'

Address personal problems early.

As the ancient Taoist life manual, the Tao Te Ching, put it, 'The great man faces problems early, so he doesn't experience them.' That advice may be thousands of years old, but it's still golden.

Once a week, spend five minutes asking yourself, 'What problems in my life might be about to develop?' Then nip them in the bud when they're easy to conquer. There's virtually no problem situation in the world that can't be effectively dealt with – if you can tackle it early enough.

Have no more than three major goals a year.

There are hundreds of 'success' books on the market telling you to make a list of scores of things you'd like to achieve, then go make them happen.

But they usually never happen, and here's the simple reason: You can only do a few things well, so much concentration and effort do they require.

Trust me, for ten years I tried to work on ten goals for the year and I only ended up getting depressed with my failures.

Pick just one big thing you'd like to achieve for the year, and maybe just two smaller things you want to do or get, then focus on those. Unless you focus your energies like a laser in one major area, success will most likely elude you.

That is the cold, hard truth.

Keep personal calls to under three minutes at work.

Try this test. For one week record in a journal how much time you waste doing unimportant jobs or talking on the phone. You'll be amazed at how much time goes down the drain on trivia.

Try to make or return personal calls before or after work – or if they're really important, at lunchtime. You'll become far more productive.

Remember, it's not just the time you're talking that you lose, it's the time it takes to get your mind back into your work *after* the call that costs you too.

Look for industries which might converge with yours.

Just like at the cellular level, were sub-atomic particles in our body are ceaselessly joining together then splitting apart, so too in business there is widespread convergence.

Petrol stations are merging with general stores. Computers will soon merge with televisions inside your home. Sport has already merged with fashion.

Is your industry in the process of convergence? If it is and you can be among the first to see it and act upon it, then a great fortune awaits.

Eat till you're only two-thirds full.

Doctors aren't certain about a lot of research, but they are certain about this:

Tests on all warm-blooded animals indicate that if we stop eating before we're full, we'll live longer.

This concurs with a major national study on centenarians in China. Researchers discovered that the vast majority of people who were over 100 years old did not eat much.[19]

Don't work past 7p.m.

Long hours are a corporate disease, and usually lead to low effectiveness and poor time management.

Most people who work late do so for two reasons. Either they've got too much work on, or they don't get enough done during the day.

In the case of the former, you've probably got too much to do because you're not focusing on the important, high-leverage activities and are instead getting caught up in minutiae.

In the case of the latter, you probably spend too much time in meetings, travelling, lunching or just plain procrastinating.

Get hard on yourself. If you can't get it done in ten hours a day, you're just not being effective.

Try this radical test: Attempt to do your entire job in four hours a day. Most people will be stunned that when push comes to shove, it can be done. Do this test and you'll never look at your usual workday the same way again.

Become friends with the boss's secretary.

Most people suck up to the boss. A better tactic is to make a sincere effort to become friends with the boss's secretary.

Senior ranking secretaries usually have a hell of a lot of power. And knowledge. Befriend them, and they'll often let you in on some of their secrets, or at least give you regular sound advice on the boss's movements and moods.

Think 80/20.

You may have heard of the 'Pareto Principle'. Invented by an Italian economist, Vilfredo Pareto,[20] it states that '80% of your results come from 20% of your actions'. That is, if you concentrate on doing that 20% of actions that really count, your chances of success will skyrocket.

Many people know of this principle, but precious few make it a major part of their life. That's disappointing, because I believe that an absolute dedication to only doing the vital 20%, in all areas of your life, will turn you into a super success.

What is the single most important thing you could do now to improve your life? Your relationship? Your business? Your health?

Do it. Then keep doing it, and watch your success skyrocket. The 80/20 rule is one of the most powerful principles in the material world: it's imperative you make it a part of the way you do things.

when they zig, you zag

Always employ too few people.

Being a little short-staffed at work makes the staff you've got work harder and really push to do their best.

Also, strangely enough, it's often the companies where the staff are really working hard that have the best team morale. Probably because most people get a real achievement and adrenalin buzz when they're giving it all they've got.

The trick, of course, is to know the difference between stretching staff levels and reaching breaking point.

Meditate.

Hardly anyone does it, but it's clinically proven to increase health, happiness and success.

Over the last 20 years, numerous studies have shown that regular daily meditation can lower stress, improve metabolism, increase calmness, and markedly improve your capacity to think clearly.

The time you'll lose daily in meditation you'll more than make up for in superior working efficiency.

Ready. Fire. Aim.

'Ready. Fire. Aim.' is the maxim of the brilliant businessman and one time presidential candidate, Ross Perot. He lives it.

Not only did he turn his first company, EDS, into a multibillion-dollar business, he then repeated the feat with his Perot Systems Corporation. His secret? Taking action before you're totally ready. Perot believes some progress is usually better than no progress. You may not be right all the time, but at the very least, you learned something.

Is there too much thinking in your life and not enough action? Reverse that situation for a month and you'll be stunned at the results.

Rush unimportant jobs.

Most of what you do at work is trivial! Only a small portion of each person's day is spent doing the truly important tasks.

If you accept that as the truth, then you'll have to agree it makes sense to get all the unimportant tasks done as quickly as possible, even if it means you do only an average job on them.

The faster you do (or even better, delegate) those trivial time wasters, the sooner you can get on to the juicy stuff.

As the world's richest investor, Warren Buffett, once remarked, 'What's not worth doing, is not worth doing well.'

Get an electronic diary.

They're much more effective than those hundred-year-old paper ones.

With an electronic diary you often get ten-years-worth of diary pages – so come December you can put in January's dates without having to buy a new diary.

You can also insert weekly meetings just by pushing a repeat button, rather than going through the hassle of writing it in each week.

If you're like me, clients are always changing appointments on you. In the old paper diary days, that meant crossing out the old appointment and writing in the new one – creating a very messy page. With an electronic diary you can just delete the old appointment, so it's much neater.

I suggest the new improved Apple Newton™ (expensive, but superb) or the internationally renowned US Robotics Palm Pilot.

Assume too good to be true deals aren't.

It's true, probably a couple of times in your life you'll get offered an incredible, no brainer way to make money.

The problem is knowing whether it's legit, because 90% of the time they aren't.

A far better way to make money is to go for good deals (not amazing ones) that require less investment and do more of them.

That way you spread your risk over a number of deals, and considerably increase your chance of making an overall profit.

Cover the downside.

When real estate tycoon Donald Trump was making a squillion in the eighties, he penned a book called *The Art Of The Deal*.

In it he listed the techniques he used to select business ventures, and paramount among these was always making sure that if a deal went wrong, he had enough money to cover the loss.

When he almost went bankrupt five years later he admitted that one of the primary reasons was that he'd abandoned this Cover the Downside rule.

Learn from Trump's mistakes. Even if your business deals aren't huge, ask yourself, 'Could I handle the situation if things went unexpectedly bad?'

If you even pause when answering this question, don't even think of doing the deal.

127

Understand the awesome power of persistence.

Want to know the single most important reason that most people don't achieve their dreams?

They give up too early.

Most people simply don't realise that consistent failure is a necessary component to achieving spectacular success. If you're not failing regularly you're either aiming too low, or not pushing yourself.

Colonel Sanders was turned down 1009 times before one restaurant bought his chicken recipe.

Walt Disney got 203 rejections from banks until one said yes to financing Disneyland.

Thomas Edison is said to have had over 10,000 separate experiments before he succeeded in creating the electric light bulb.

The secret to success is persistence, persistence, persistence, persistence, persistence, persistence, persistence, persistence, persistence, persistence!

But make sure it's intelligent persistence – vary your methods, be flexible, think laterally. Then keep on going and going until finally success eventually gives in and gives you what you rightly deserve.

Invest 10% of your income.

According to statistics, 85% of people who retire do not have enough money to live unsupported by the government.

Why? Not because they never earned enough, but usually because they spent all their money instead of investing it. They lived for today and forgot about tomorrow, until one day tomorrow came up and bit them on the behind!

Learn from the mistakes of the mediocre. Invest 10% of your income now, even if you think you can't afford to. Take the pain now and you'll have decades of pleasure in your sunset years. Spend it all now and your final decades could be very uncomfortable indeed.

Work with urgency

Remember Parkinson's Law – work expands to fill the time allotted to it. In other words, when you've got lots of time you use it all, and when you've got only a little time you somehow get the job completed anyway.

Why do we usually complete the task even if we have a shortage of time? Primarily because when we push ourselves, we think a lot faster and act a lot faster.

This being the case, it makes a lot of sense to create 'false urgency' whenever you're at work. By setting short deadlines on most tasks you'll be amazed at how much you can get done in a week.

Urgency works, and is a crucial weapon in any top performer's armoury.

Understand the elements of negotiation.

According to Herb Cohen, one of the world's greatest negotiators, the three crucial areas of any negotiation are Power, Time and Information. Your understanding of each will determine your success in a negotiation.[21]

Power: How much power does the person you're negotiating with have? How much do they think you have? How much do you have that they need, and vice versa?

Time: Do they have an urgent deadline? Do you? How far away is it? Do they have time to look at other options?

Information: How much do you know about their situation? Their motivations? How much do they know of yours? When should you reveal yours to them?

When going into an important negotiation, even if it's just with your landlord, keep these three crucial variables in mind. Your knowledge of them may well decide who comes out on top.

Place your alarm clock away from your bed.

How many times have you switched your alarm clock off and gone straight back to sleep? Too many to count, I'll bet.

I've probably arrived late or missed at least ten major meetings or events because of my snoozing habits. But then I came up with the answer.

By simply putting your alarm clock on the other side of the room, you'll always be up out of bed within seconds. By the time you've walked across your bedroom to turn the darn thing off you're well and truly awake.

Works every time . . .

Understand international business lag.

A lot of people have made their fortunes taking a good product or business concept from one country to another.

This is because even in this age of globalisation, it's often years before good ideas spread to other countries.

Take advantage of this lag time. Next time you're on vacation overseas, keep an eye out for products or services that would be a big hit in your own country.

The world is full of people who have made millions, and even billions, using this technique.

Commit to a direction, any direction.

The biggest reason people don't succeed is that they're too scared to commit to a course of action.

They give up on jobs easily, they procrastinate on career choices, they change their minds on even minor issues constantly. As a result, what action they do eventually take is half hearted and consequently ineffective.

Don't know which way to go? Just choose, and then commit to it 100% for a year. *Then* stop and see if you took the right path. Sure you'll make mistakes, but over the course of a lifetime you'll end up far ahead of those who never commit to anything.

Always keep a note pad with you.

Ever come up with a great idea, and then forgotten it before you wrote it down? Me too, numerous times.

The trick to not losing these gems of inspiration is to always carry a small pad and pen. That way, when you have a good thought, you can quickly jot it down on the spot.

The founder of IMG, the largest sports management company in the world, is Mark McCormack. Mark uses this same method, but instead of carrying a small pad, he keeps some small white cards in his pocket. Quite often he pens down some thoughts and gives them straight to one of his staff.

Me? I keep a tiny digital recorder under my car seat. Any ideas I have while driving I just record then and there, then give the device to my PA when I arrive at work.

Watch for company announcements in the press.

You'd be amazed at how many corporations reveal to the press their great new business ideas. Often, if you act fast, you can beat them to market with an idea they thought of!

In fact, one of the world's richest men used this technique to build his fortune.

The founder of Oracle, the second biggest software company in the world, is Larry Ellison. One morning Larry read in the newspaper that IBM was about to develop a new kind of business software.

Ellison thought it was a great idea, so good in fact he did it himself, before IBM could get their act together. The result? Ellison is now the fifth wealthiest man in America, with an estimated wealth of over $6 billion . . .

Remember that begun is half done.

Why don't most people achieve much in life?

Because they can't bring themselves to
take action. When faced with major tasks or
obstacles they frequently procrastinate and
avoid tackling them head on. Then after a
while they get frustrated with their lack of
progress and give up.

I too have suffered from procrastination,
and occasionally still do. But it's far less of a
problem since I learned a simple but
brilliantly effective way to handle it.

When faced with an unpleasant task, just begin it, even if it's just for 10 or 20 minutes. It's easy to do almost anything for a short period of time, and once you start it a funny thing happens. You often realise doing the chore is not nearly so irksome as you thought, and usually you continue working on the task for one hour, two hours, sometimes even the whole day.

But even if you do stop working on the job after 20 minutes, you've at least made some progress, and you'll have less to do tomorrow.

Think Big!

If I were to choose the one fundamental difference between people who achieve enormous things and those who don't, it's thinking big.

History has proven that most achievers choose to have big dreams and pursue them with gusto. Sometimes they doubted themselves, sometimes they wanted to give in, but ultimately they stuck by their audacious dreams.

Gandhi had the outrageous dream that he could gain India's independence without violence, and achieved it. Henry Ford envisioned a world where the horse and buggy was replaced by mechanical transporters known as cars, and made it happen. Bill Gates dreamed of a computer on every desk in the nation, and his dream too is fast becoming fact.

Are you thinking big enough?

Dream big, reader, dream big. It is the first step to magnificent achievement.

Does dreaming big ensure big success? Of course not. But, as the Persian proverb goes, 'Not everyone who chased the zebra caught it, but he who caught it chased after it.'

Go for it!

REFERENCES

1   *Super Learning 2000* by S Ostrander and L Schroder, Souvenir Press, 1994.

2   *Eat To Win* by Dr Robert Haas, Signet Books, 1985.

3   *The Secrets of Longevity* by Professor S Talalas and J Talalas, Hill of Content Publishing, 1997.

4   Pocket Books (Simon & Schuster), 1969.

5   *Musclemag International*, Schwarzenegger Special Edition, 1997.

6   For more time-saving tips, see his book, *How To Get Control of Your Time and Your Life*, Signet Books, 1974.

7   A good one is *Feng Shui. The Chinese Art of Placement* by Sarah Rossbach, Arkana, 1983.

8   For more idea generation techniques, read the works of lateral thinking supremo, Edward de Bono.

9   *The Secrets of Longevity*, ibid.

10 *Psycho Nutrition. How to Control Your Moods with Foods* by Dr William Vayda, Lothian Publishing, 1992.

11 *Brain Longevity* by Dr Dharma Singh Khalsa, Random House, 1997.

12 *American Journal of Epidemiology*, 1992, Vol 135, pp.749–62.

13 *Psycho Nutrition* ibid.

14 *Timeless Healing* by Dr Robert Benson, Hodder Headline.

15 *Brain Longevity*, ibid.

16 Random House, Australia, 1992.

17 'Black Belt for the Mind' seminar, Sydney, February, 1998.

18 *Unlimited Power* by Anthony Robbins, Fireside (Simon & Schuster), 1997.

19 See *Mystery of Longevity* by Liu Zhengcai, Foreign Language Press, Beijing.

20 *The 80–20 Principle* by Richard Koch, Nicholas Brearley Publishing, 1997.

21 *You Can Negotiate Anything* by Herb Cohen, Bantam Books, 1982.

Siimon Reynolds
Become Happy in Eight Minutes

Everybody wants to be happy.

In six basic steps, advertising ace Siimon Reynolds
combines philosophical, motivational and scientific
techniques you can use to actually make yourself feel
happy, fast.

This is *not* hype. These are *not* mind games. Use these
techniques properly and it is physiologically impossible
not to get into a better mood. They are based on
decades of research on how the brain works. They'll
work for the young, they'll work for the old. You truly are
only ever eight minutes away from feeling happy.

Isn't that a lovely thought?

Marilyn Diamond & Dr Donald Burton Schnell
Fitonics For Life

Take charge of your weight, health and happiness!

FITONICS FOR LIFE is a dynamic new prescription for total wellness. Marilyn Diamond, co-author of FIT FOR LIFE and her new partner, Dr Donald Burton Schnell, expand the FIT FOR LIFE message with the breakthrough concept of High-Energy Eating, a revolutionary approach to healthy and comfortable weight-loss.

To complete the total fitness program, FITONICS FOR LIFE includes Bodytonics: a hassle-free, twelve-minute daily natural routine of movements which tone, condition and reshape your body, and Mindtonics: an inspiring, self-constructive thinking process that is the indispensable key to health, weight-loss and happiness.

Incorporating the latest scientific findings on nutritious food, effective exercise and healthy thinking, FITONICS FOR LIFE will give you abundant energy, vibrant good health and a new zest for living.

Susie O'Neill
Choose To Win

'Sink or swim. There comes a time when everyone has a choice of giving up or persevering and making it work. Just after my heat swim in Atlanta, my coach Scott handed me a piece of paper. It read: *One of the greatest pleasures in life is achieving things that people say can't be done.* **It listed Australia's last ten individual swimming gold medalists. Alongside 1996 were the words:** *Who will be next?'*

In 1996 Susie O'Neill became the first Australian woman to win an Olympic swimming gold medal in 16 years when she captured the 200m butterfly title. Fulfilling her dream in Atlanta was the result of hard work and unshaken belief in herself in the face of pressures at the highest level.

In CHOOSE TO WIN Susie talks about the highs and lows of her extraordinary swimming career. On her path to gold she has overcome each hurdle using specific methods of motivational thinking, confidence-building and goal-setting.

CHOOSE TO WIN is not only a fascinating insight into one of Australia's greatest swimmers, it is also essential reading for anyone who faces challenges. Susie's down-to-earth, pragmatic strategies will show you how to confront any obstacle – and make your choice to win.

John Gray, PH.D.
Mars and Venus Starting Over:
A Guide to Recreating a Lasting and Loving
Relationship

John Gray, author of the history-making publishing
phenomenon, MEN ARE FROM MARS, WOMEN ARE
FROM VENUS, addresses the particular relationship
concerns of those who are starting over – newly single
after a death, divorce, or other serious breakup.

In his previous mega-bestsellers John has shown the
differences between men's and women's desires and
expectations in a relationship. He has led us through the
trials of dating, to the joys and conflicts of marriage, and
even into the privacy and pleasure of the bedroom.

Everybody wants a love that will last forever. But for
many reasons, relationships end. The healing process
after such a loss can be difficult, but getting past the
grief, anger and pain can be much easier with expert
help. Now John Gray offers comfort and empowering
advice on how to overcome loss and gain the
confidence to engage in new relationships. He instructs
readers how to move past the pain, how to recognise
when they're ready to try again, and how to negotiate
the new dating frontier. For millions of newly single
people, MARS AND VENUS STARTING OVER is like a
lifeguard at the dating pool!